Living for God while in Prison

THE PHYSICAL AND MENTAL PRISON

written by:

Alphonso Stephenson

and

Alphonso Stephenson Jr

TABLE OF Contents

chapter

1

THE CHALLENGE YOU FACE BEING IN PRISON AND LIVING FOR GOD

THE PHYSICAL OR MENTAL PRISON

²³ For all have sinned and fall short of the glory of God.
- Romans 3:23 NIV

Every human on this earth is a sinner. One day we all will die, condemned for repeatably breaking God's commands (his laws). Without Jesus, there would be no hope, but thanks to God - who has declared us not guilty because of Jesus Christ who has offered us freedom from sin and gave us the power to serve him and do his will – we have hope.

²⁴And all are justified freely by his grace through the redemption that came by Christ Jesus. -Romans 3:24 NIV

Before I turned my life around, I was in a rebellious stage of my life. Although I had two parents in the house, I was hanging out with the wrong crowd. I started to smoke, doing drugs, stealing, and I even joined a gang. My father said that if I put myself in a bad situation by hanging out with the wrong crowd, and If I got arrested, do not call him. I thought he was joking, but when I got locked up and call him, he told me he was not getting me out because of my rebelling and disobeying him, and that I must pay the consequence of choosing what I had done.

²⁰Children, obey your parents in everything,
for this pleases the Lord. -Colossians 3:20 NIV

I have been in prison for over 14 years now. Since my time in confinement, I have turned my life around, and now I have a new perspective in life through my Lord and savior, Jesus Christ. God, Himself, came to the earth in human form as Jesus Christ for the restoration and salvation of sinners. We all stand guilty as charged, and we all have missed the mark, but because he loves us so much, he sent his only Son to die in our place and give us a way out of eternal death.

¹⁶For God so loved the world that he gave his one and only Son,
that whoever believes in him shall not perish but have eternal life.
¹⁷For God did not send his Son into the world to condemn the
world, but to save the world through him. -John 3:16-17.

Jesus' sacrificial death on the cross was the penalty for sin that opened the door for humanity to receive forgiveness and redemption from it. He is not content that only a few would have access to salvation but everyone. *⁹The Lord is not slow in keeping his promise, as some understand slowness. Instead, he is patient with you, not wanting anyone to perish, but everyone to come to repentance. -2 Peter 3:9 NIV.*

3

Now you are at this point in your life where something is missing and you can feel it deep in your heart. *So, as the Holy Spirit says: 'Today, if you hear his voice, do not harden your hearts as you did in the rebellion, during the time of testing in the wilderness.'* -Hebrews 3:7-8 NIV.

Today, repent and trust Jesus, and God will give you eternal life as a gift. But you do not know how to provide you with the heart to God. It is straightforward. The bible says that *If you declare with your mouth, 'Jesus is Lord,' and believe in your heart that God raised him from the dead, you will be saved. 10 For it is with your heart that you believe and are justified, and it is with your mouth that you profess your faith and are saved. -Romans 10:9-10 NIV 13, For everyone who calls on the name of the Lord will be saved. -Romans 10:13 NIV,*

You can give your life to God and be saved anywhere, any time, and any place. All you must do is ask the Lord to come into your heart and acknowledge that you are a sinner and ask God to forgive you for all your sins, *If we confess our sins, he is faithful and just and will forgive us our sins and purify us from all unrighteousness. -1 John 1:9 NI.* Ask him to create a clean heart and restore the proper Spirit within you. cleanse you from all

4

unrighteousness, and lastly to be your Lord and savior. *¹⁰Create in me a pure heart, O God, and renew a steadfast spirit within me.* -Psalm 51:10 NIV,

At this point in your life, you are saved, and now you are a new believer. Grace saves you through your faith, but the evidence of your faith is in response to you repenting. *⁸For it is by grace you have been saved, through faith—and this is not from yourselves, it is the gift of God— ⁹not by works, so that no one can boast.* -Ephesians 2:8-9 NIV.

I may be in prison, but I am free because I have Jesus in my life. A lot of inmates are in a physical and mental prison because of their mindset. Some people are accessible in the world, walking around, but their minds are in jail because they put their hope and trust in man as governed by society. The only way to freedom is when you put all you have in the only person that can set you free, and that person is Jesus Christ. *³⁶So if the Son sets you free, you will be free indeed.* -John 8:36 NIV

Most people live their entire lives in prison, not physically but mentally, a mental prison of their own making; they will be

emotionally sensitive or reactive. Being in mental prison is when you judge yourself harshly by thinking you are ugly, stupid, and lazy, thinking there is something wrong with you. When your start to judge others or the world and people in a negative light. *7Do not judge, or you too will be judged. 2 For in the same way you judge others, you will be judged, and with the measure you use, it will be measured to you. -Matthew 7:1-2 NIV*

Fear is a powerful emotion that keeps you in a mental prison. Fear will replace your peace and imprison you with doubt. You are afraid of succeeding in life or a change for a better life. *5Trust in the LORD with all your heart and lean not on your understanding; 6in all your ways acknowledge him, and he will make your paths straight. 7Do not be wise in your own eyes; fear the LORD and shun evil. 8This will bring health to your body and nourishment to your bones. -Proverbs 3:5-8 NIV*

Unforgiveness is an emotion that keeps you in a mental prison. Unforgiveness takes up a lot of mental space. It affects your judgment and perspective because you view the world and yourself through the lens of hurt. It affects our character and integrity; it does not bring out the best in us. Unforgiveness builds a wall

between you and God. ³¹ *Get rid of all bitterness, rage, and anger, brawling, and slander, along with every form of malice.* ³² *Be kind and compassionate to one another, forgiving each other, just as in Christ God forgave you. -Ephesians 4:31-32 NIV*

chapter

2

Without Truth, there is no Grace and Mercy

¹⁷For the law was given through Moses; grace and Truth came through Jesus Christ. -John 1:17 NIV

Truth – what is accurate and agrees with reality.

Grace – God's unmerited favor and love lead Him to grant salvation to the believer through the exercise of their faith in Jesus Christ.

Mercy – giving or receiving care when it's not deserved; compassion for others.

The Truth is the word of God, and the terms of God are Truth. His word will never lie because God is Truth. *Jesus says, 'I am the way, the Truth, and the life. No one come to the Father except through me.' -John 14:6 NIV*

Everyone who comes to Jesus must come to Him in Truth because Jesus is Truth. The word of God is Truth; whatever he says is Truth, and his word will never come back to us void. If he says that we are blessed and anything you ask of him, he will provide, then that is what we must believe and stand on because his word is Truth, and there is no way that Jesus can lie. *¹⁹God is*

not a man that he should lie; neither the son of man, that he should repent: hath he said, and shall he not do it? Or hath he spoken, and shall he not make it good? -Numbers 23:19 KJV

When we come to Jesus, we must come in Truth, letting him know that we need his help because everyone has fallen short of the glory of God and deserves God's justice. However, God's justice is satisfied and His Truth upheld through the sacrifice of Jesus on the cross. That act delivers God's grace to those who will accept it in faith. Now you can ask for his forgiveness; when that happens, His Grace will be upon you. That means that now he will give you time to get yourself right before He brings judgment upon you. And after he shows you grace, then mercy comes into play by not giving you the punishment you deserve because you have come to him in Truth. Grace and Truth brought salvation, moving us by the kindness of God to turn to him for the mercy we need so badly.

When you trust Jesus, you are free from the condemnation of the law. We become one with him and now at perfect peace with our Father. Even though you still wrestle with sin in your life and often fail, you are no longer condemned for the sake of Jesus.

As a believer, we must relate to the Truth in everything we do.

We must know it. *⁶Behold, thou desire Truth in the inward parts, And in the hidden part, thou shalt make me to know wisdom.* -Psalm 51:6 KJV

We must seek it. *⁵Go up and down the streets of Jerusalem, look around and consider, search through her squares, if you can find but one person who deals honestly and seeks the truth, I will forgive this city.* -Jeremiah 5:1 NIV

We must choose it. *³⁰I have chosen the way of faithfulness; I have set my heart on your laws.* -Psalm 119:30 NIV

We must believe it. *¹³If we are faithless, He remains faithful, for he cannot disown himself.* -2 Timothy 2:13 NIV

We must love it. *¹⁹This is what the LORD Almighty says: 'The fasts of the fourth, fifth, seventh and tenth months will become joyful and glad occasions and happy festivals for Judah. Therefore, love, Truth , and peace.'* -Zechariah 8:19 NIV

We must walk in it. *³"for I have always been mindful of your unfailing love and have lived in reliance on your faithfulness.* -Psalm 26:3 NIV

We must live by it. _²¹But whoever lives by the Truth comes into the light, so that it may be seen plainly that what they have done has been done in the sight of God. -John 3:21 NIV_

We must obey it. _⁷You were running a good race. Who cut in on you to keep you from obeying the Truth? -Galatians 5:7 NIV_

We must worship in it. _²³"Yet a time is coming and has now come when the true worshipers will worship the Father in the Spirit and in Truth, for they are the kind of worshipers the Father seeks. 24 God is spirit, and his worshipers must worship in the Spirit and in Truth. -John 4:23-24 NIV_

We must speak it. _²⁵Therefore each of you must put off falsehood and speak truthfully to your neighbor, for we are all members of one body. -Ephesians 4:25 NIV_

After you relate to the Truth then, the Truth will:

Protect you. _¹¹Do not withhold your mercy from me, LORD; may your love and faithfulness always protect me. -Psalm 40:11 NIV_

Guides you. _³Send me your light and your faithful care, let them lead me; let them bring me to your holy mountain, to the place where you dwell. -Psalm 43:3 NIV_

Set you free. *³¹To the Jews who had believed him, Jesus said, 'If you hold to my teaching, you are really my disciples. ³²Then you will know the Truth, and the Truth will set you free.' -John 8:31-32 NIV*

Sanctifies you. *¹⁷Sanctify them by the truth; your word is truth. -John 17:17 NIV*

Purifies you. *²²Now that you have purified yourselves by obeying the truth so that you have sincere love for each other, love one another deeply, from the heart. -1 Peter 1:22 NIV*

Grace does not stop once you get saved; God is gracious to us for the rest of our lives, working within and upon us. God word has given us the example of God grace: Grace justifies us before God. *²⁴ and all are justified freely by his grace through the redemption that came by Christ Jesus. -Romans 3:24 NIV*

Grace provides us access to God as we communicate in prayer and have fellowship with Him. *⁶to the praise of his glorious grace, which he has freely given us in the One he loves. -Ephesians 1:6 NIV*

Grace gives us a new relationship of intimacy with God. *¹⁷"And the Lord said to Moses, 'I will do the very thing you have asked*

because I am pleased with you, and I know you by name.'" -Exodus 33:17 NIV

Grace disciplines and trains us to live in a way that honors God. *[11] For the grace of God has appeared that offers salvation to all people. [12] It teaches us to say 'No' to ungodliness and worldly passions, and to live self-controlled, upright and godly lives in this present age, [13] while we wait for the blessed hope—the appearing of the glory of our great God and Savior, Jesus Christ, [14] who gave himself for us to redeem us from all wickedness and to purify for himself a people that are his very own, eager to do what is good. -Titus 2:11–14 NIV*

Grace grants us spiritual riches. *[22] The blessing of the LORD makes one rich, and He adds no sorrow with it. -Proverbs 10:22 NIV*

Grace helps you in your everyday needs. *[16] Let us then approach God's throne of grace with confidence, so that we may receive mercy and find grace to help us in our time of need. -Hebrews 4:16 NIV*

Grace is the reason for our every deliverance. *[6] I put no trust in my bow, my sword does not bring me victory; [7] but you give us victory over our enemies, you put our adversaries to shame. [8] In God we make our boast all day long, and we will praise your name forever. -Psalm 44:6–8 NIV*

Grace preserves us, comforts us, encourages us, and strengthens us. *¹⁴May the grace of the Lord Jesus Christ, and the love of God, and the fellowship of the Holy Spirit be with you all. -2 Corinthians 13:14 NIV*

Grace is actively and continually working in the lives of all believers. The mercy of God is undeserved kindness and compassion that he gives to all believer, the mercy of God is part of his nature:

God is merciful. *³¹For the Lord , your God, is a merciful God; he will not abandon or destroy you or forget the covenant with your ancestors, which he confirmed to them by oath. -Deuteronomy 4:31 NIV*

God exercises mercy freely. *¹⁵For he says to Moses, 'I will have mercy on whom I have mercy, and I will have compassion on whom I have compassion.' ¹⁶It does not, therefore, depend on human desire or effort but on God's mercy. ¹⁷For Scripture says to Pharaoh: 'I raised you up for this very purpose, that I might display my power in you and that my name might be proclaimed in all the earth.' ¹⁸Therefore, God has mercy on whom he wants to have mercy, and he hardens whom he wants to harden. -Romans 9:15-18 NIV*

God's mercy triumphs over judgment. *¹³because judgment without mercy will be shown to anyone who has not been merciful. Mercy triumphs over judgment. -James 2:13 NIV*

God expression of his mercy through his:

Forgiving our sins. *¹Have mercy on me, O God, according to your unfailing love; according to your great compassion blot out my transgressions. ²Wash away all my iniquity and cleanse me from my sin. -Psalm 51:1-2NIV*

Saving us in Christ. *⁴But because of his great love for us, God, who is rich in mercy, ⁵made us alive with Christ even when we were dead in transgressions—it is by grace you have been saved. -Ephesians 2:4-5 NIV*

Receiving us back to himself. *¹²Go, proclaim this message toward the north: 'Return, faithless Israel,' declares the Lord., 'I will frown on you no longer, for I am faithful,' declares the Lord , 'I will not be angry forever. ¹³Only acknowledge your guilt, you have rebelled against the Lord your God, you have scattered your favors to foreign gods under every spreading tree, and have not obeyed me,' declares the Lord . Jeremiah 3:12-13 NIV*

Heal you. *²⁷Indeed, he was ill and almost died. But God had mercy on him, and not on him only but also on me, to spare me sorrow upon sorrow. -Philippians 2:27 NIV*

Keep you safe from your enemy. *⁹The Lord has heard my cry for mercy; the Lord accepts my prayer. ¹⁰All my enemies will be overwhelmed with shame and anguish; they will turn back and suddenly be put to shame. -Psalm 6:9-10 NIV*

Truth, Grace, and Mercy are a part of Jesus Character. Jesus' character demonstrates the perfect balance of both grace and Truth. He is "full" of both. If we believe in the Father, Son, and Holy Spirit, we must know that the word of God is Truth, and we are all sinner, and the only thing that is keeping us right now is Jesus Grace and Mercy because of the love that he has for us.

It is hard to live for Christ while in confinement with so many outside influences discouraging your belief, corrupting your walk with lies of personal fantasies. I remember one time when one inmate was asking me:

Inmate: "Why do you believe in Jesus?"

Me: "Why shouldn't I believe in God? I didn't create myself, or did you?"

Inmate: "A lot of religions come from the east where they believe that the supreme consciousness of the world said I am alone, let me create people to populate this world."

Me: At this point, I knew that this conversation wasn't going to be a debate, so I tried to change the subject, *⁴Do not answer a fool according to his folly, or you yourself will be just like him. ⁵Answer a fool according to his folly, or he will be wise in his own eyes. -Proverbs 26:4-5 NIV*

I tried to change the subject by saying, "Yeah, you are right with your sarcasm," but I know that God is going to bring me out of prison.

Inmate: "Man, I'm just saying all of you Christians believe in some spook in the sky that's supposed to fulfill some promise of luxury when you die. That's so naïve; what if it's all a lie."

Me: "We believe by faith, we talk to him in prayer, we wait for his answer, and then watch and see His works manifest in you. It's amazing to see His Word come true; it's terrific."

Inmate: "But that's the point. It is all coming true because you believe in it. The world is a magical place. If you view things

negatively, then you are going to experience life negatively, but if you have an optimistic view of life, then all is good."

Me: "Isn't God good?"

Inmate: "Man, have you ever read the Vedas?" (he asks sternly)

Vedas means "knowledge," are the oldest texts of Hinduism. They are derived from the ancient Indo-Aryan culture of the Indian Subcontinent and began as an oral tradition that was passed down through generations before finally being written in Vedic Sanskrit between 1500 and 500 BCE (Before Common Era).

Me: "I had not." (I just heard about it.) It was the oldest spiritual scripture, but it had nothing to do with the bible. The bible is the book for me. It stands alone with the Word of God." (The BIBLE, I sang) "The bible is whatever you need to broaden your horizon and open your mind to a better outlook on life, so stop being ignorant."

Inmate: "I'm not ignorant."

Me: "God's words are here in front of me. (I was pointing to the bible) "You are telling me about God and some Vedas."

Inmate: "Come on, man, stop being stupid. Don't you think there is more to life than what meets the eyes? If you are hungry for knowledge, there are other books out there to tell you whatever you need to know about life."

Me: "But I don't want to read other books about life. The bible is all I need."

Inmate: "But you have to. It's like this, looking at this object from your point of view and describing it, and me looking at the same object; but who can say who's right or wrong, and this is how God looks at it."

Me: "Well, I know there are other books out there, but they are not telling me about my Lord and Savior, my soul, or about redemption."

Inmate: "Why do you believe in all that dogma?"

Me: "Because I can see it and feel it and test it in prayer. I talk to God, and I ask him to show me things and help me. I read His Word and try to imitate his prophets to strengthen my faith. It's all tried and true. That's why I believe."

Inmate: "You are crazy like crazy glue."

Me: "Don't you know that God lives in you and me. He loves you no matter what you have done; that is the reason why He sent his only Son to die for humankind so we can be saved from eternal death and be with him for eternity. Thank you, Lord."

One of the obstacles I faced while in prison is mainly because the devil does not want me to serve God. The devil wanted me to be the way I was and keep doing the things that brought me there in the first place.

The devil does not care anything about you. His job is to steal you away from God, to kill you internally by using your flesh against you, and to destroy you spiritually. But Jesus, your redeemer, came so that you may have life and have it to the fullest. *¹⁰The thief comes only to steal and kill and destroy; I have come that they may have life and have it to the full. -John 10:10 NIV*

While my body is in a physical prison, my mind is not because I am put my hope in Christ Jesus, not in man, because man as let me down time and time again. Since I have given my life to God, that is where my hope lies because *¹³May the God of hope fill you*

with all joy and peace as you trust in him, so that you may overflow with hope by the power of the Holy Spirit. -Romans 15:13 NIV.

So, what is hope? Hope is a sure and steady faith in God's promises. A firm expectation of the future, solid, not moved easily, and rooted.

You should know two things: the first one is God gives us hope, and the second is that hope comes through the Holy Spirit. Without hope, your life loses its meaning, and your hope must be rooted in God and God's promises through his word. As Christian/believer, your hope in God's promises should be for:

Righteousness. *⁵For through the Spirit we eagerly await by faith the righteousness for which we hope. -Galatians 5:5 NIV*

Salivation. *⁸"But since we belong to the day, let us be sober, putting on faith and love as a breastplate, and the hope of salvation as a helmet. -1 Thessalonians 5:8 NIV.*

Resurrection. *⁶And now it is because of my hope in what God has promised our ancestors that I am on trial today. ⁷This is the promise our twelve tribes are hoping to see fulfilled as they earnestly serve*

God day and night. King Agrippa, it is because of this hope that these Jews are accusing me. -Acts 26:6-7 NIV.

Eternal Life. *[19]If only for this life we have hope in Christ, we are of all people most to be pitied. [20]But Christ has indeed been raised from the dead, the first fruits of those who have fallen asleep. [21]For since death came through a man, the resurrection of the dead comes also through a man. [22]For as in Adam all die, so in Christ all will be made alive. [23]But each in turn: Christ, the first fruits; then, when he comes, those who belong to him. [24]Then the end will come when he hands over the kingdom to God the Father after he has destroyed all dominion, authority, and power. [25]For he must reign until he has put all his enemies under his feet. -1 Corinthians 15:19-25 NIV.*

When you put your hope in God, it produces joy and peace through the Holy Spirit's power. Everyone has hope, and society calls hope and wishful thinking, but believers hope it is in God's promises. The difference between the world hope and Christian hope. *[12]Hope deferred makes the heart sick, but a longing fulfilled is a tree of life. -Proverbs 13:12 NIV*

When you put your hope in man, it will make you sick when it does not happen, but when you put your hope in God, you will

find a life fill with joy, and He will never disappoint you. *⁸It is better to trust in the Lord than to put confidence in man. -Psalm 118:8 NIV.*

Without God, there is no hope *¹²in order that we, who were the first to put our hope in Christ, might be for the praise of his glory." -Ephesians 1:12 NIV;* Our hope is linked with Faith, Trust, and Expectation. *²⁰I eagerly expect and hope that I will in no way be ashamed but will have sufficient courage so that now as always Christ will be exalted in my body, whether by life or by death. -Philippians 1:20 NIV*

Hope to give you patience. *²⁴Now that we are saved, we eagerly look forward to this freedom, for if you already have something, you don't need to hope for it. ²⁵But if we look forward to something we don't have yet, we must wait patiently and confidently. -Romans 8:24-25 NIV*

One thing that my hope in God will give me is patience for Eternal life; this is one thing I am not going to rush. We must live in expectation every day, having faith and trusting in God's words. *¹³Therefore, with minds that are alert and fully sober, set*

your hope on the grace to be brought to you when Jesus Christ is revealed at his coming. -1 Peter 1:13 NIV

Ask yourself this question, do I have the *world hope* (hope in man) or do I have *Christian hope* (in God's promise)?

One of the most noticeable moment that I face while in confinement is having self-control, another reason why self-control is so necessary for your walk with Christ.

Inmate: "Alphonso, do you understand what it means to be a Christian? Now take me, for example. I have been a Christian for years now, and I believe I have figured out what it means to be a Christian."

Me: "I do, but some people do not understand what it truly means to be a Christian."

Inmate: "I go to service and I sing in the prison choir. I do believe I know what it means to be a Christian. Oh, and to prove my point even further, I even have Jesus in my life, just like the preacher said we need."

Me: "I think there is a little more to it than that."

Inmate: "What do you mean; all this stuff makes us great Christians."

Me: "No, the thing that makes us Christians is, you have to be saved and accept Jesus Christ as your Lord and Savior and serve Him with your heart by faith, not with your deeds, and not any of this other stuff."

Inmate: "Well, yeah, there is that, but I do have Jesus in my life."

Me: "OK, but have you given your heart to him? And what has he done in your life lately?"

Inmate: (looking a bit confused) "What has he done in my life lately? Well, there he is; every day, he is right here."

He pointed to his bible on the shelf.

Me: I know, but that still does not answer my question."

Inmate: "What in the world are you saying? I do have Him in my life; I mean, he is right over there every day, right there. What are you doing? Get back over here."

I walked over to his bookshelf and took his bible from the shelf, and started to explain to him.

Me: "God has been a part of your life, and only as a part of your life. He wants to be your life. God wants to walk with you in everything that you do. You see, He does not want to be just your top priority; he wants to be all your priorities. There is so much more to Christianity than just going to church service here and being a part of the person choir. God wants you and me to be holy. See, you are missing out on so much that God can offer you, and you are missing out by putting him in a little corner of your life. If you would only let Him into all your heart, He will show you the joy that comes through following Him. I know God is tired of just being a reference point in your life. He wants to be your friend, your father, your Lord. It is time that you learn what it means to be a Christian. It is time to let God take control of your life. Trust God; he will not let you down because that is a promise He made to us."

chapter

3

HAVING
SELF-CONTROL

⁵For this very reason, make every effort to add to your faith goodness; and to goodness, knowledge; ⁶and to knowledge, self-control; and to self-control, perseverance; and to perseverance, godliness; ⁷and to godliness, mutual affection; and to mutual affection, love. -2 Peter 1:5-7 NIV

Self-control- the ability to control oneself, one's emotion and desires, and Their expression in one behavior, especially in a difficult situation.

What is self-control? When people talk about self-control, they talk about control your anger, but I am talking about the spiritual part of self-control, which deals with your flesh and the ability to say no to your fleshly desires.

Self-control's spiritual meaning is to restrain one's emotion, action, and desires and be in harmony with God's will. Self-control is doing God's will and not living for yourself. It is impossible to please God and live a godly life without self-control. We all can have self-control just like Jesus had, but we must depend on the Holy Spirit to guide us, no matter what is going on around us.

The Holy Spirit, with help you with self-control from doing the wrong thing and to do the right thing. *¹¹For the Grace of God*

has appeared that offers salvation to all people. ¹²It teaches us to say
'No' to ungodliness and worldly passions, and to live self-controlled,
upright and godly lives in this present age. -Titus 2:11-12 NIV

Self-control helps us to resist temptation and avoid confronting the things of this world. Showing control will help to guide your decisions because your sinful nature will lead you into temptation without self-control. Self-control is often a matter of responding rather than reacting. Responding means saying things positively or negatively, while reacting means behaving in a particular way when responding to something; In a positive or a negative way. Reacting is emotional while responding is emotional intelligence.

When you react to a situation, you are letting your emotions take control and, more likely, you become defensive and say hurtful words, being aggressive in the situation.

When you respond, you will have a thoughtful response guided by reason more than emotion. Jesus is the perfect example of self-control because He allows the Holy Spirit to guide and lead him; that is why he possesses all the fruits of the spirits. *²²But the fruit of the Spirit is love, joy, peace, forbearance, kindness, goodness,*

faithfulness, ²³gentleness and self-control. Against such things there is no law. -Galatians 5:22-23 NIV

Jesus not only came to die for your sins but to be the example of how to live a Godly and sinless life; he was the example of how things were before Adams disobeyed God and brought sin into the world. *¹²Therefore, just as sin entered the world through one man, and death through sin, and in this way, death came to all people, because all sinned. -Romans 5:12 NIV*

Self-control affects the whole person, from the physical to the mental part and even to your speech. *¹⁹My dear brothers and sisters, take note of this: Everyone should be quick to listen, slow to speak, and slow to become angry, ²⁰because human anger does not produce the righteousness that God desires. ²¹Therefore, get rid of all moral filth and the evil that is so prevalent and humbly accept the word planted in you, which can save you. -James 1:19-21 NIV*

The Word of God says that you should be quick to listen because when you are talking too much, you are not listening to what the other person needs to tell you. Once you have made your statement, give the person the time to respond. While the person is talking, you must listen to everything they are saying,

31

not just what you want to hear or while picking out certain words. That way, you will not react out of anger and say things you later regret. *²¹The tongue has the power of life and death, and those who love it will eat its fruit. -Proverbs 18:21 NIV*

One of the most challenging assignments for Christians is self-control of the mind. The human mind is an incredible creation that God has given us. Now we can choose right from wrong to serve the Lord or the devil. How you think determines how you live and your behavior as a believer; that is why we must *²Set your mind on things above, not on earthly thing. -Colossians 3:2 NIV.* Self-control begins by avoiding the dangerous situation altogether when possible. Take a stand on your beliefs. If you lack self-control, ask God to help you. He is there to help.

Without self-control, you open yourself for the enemy to attack you; you will be like a hole in a wall that should protects a city. That wall will keep the enemy from gaining a foothold over you. *²⁸Like a city whose walls are broken through is a person who lacks self-control. -Proverbs 25:28 NIV*

When you exercise self-control, you take captive of every negative thought and make it obedient to the Word of God. What you

are doing is setting your mind on things above and not on earthly things *⁵We demolish arguments and every pretension that sets itself up against the knowledge of God, and we take captive every thought to make it obedient to Christ.* -2 Corinthians 10:5 NIV

Self-control is a fruit that will grow in you when you continually choose to die to your flesh and live righteously. As a Christian, you have the Holy Spirit in you, who gives you the strength to stand up and say no to temptation because you do not have the power or ability to choose what is right, especially when it does not feel good.

You serve a God that is full of Grace, faithfulness, and mercy, and who will work wonders in your weakness. *⁹But he said to me, 'My grace is sufficient for you, for my power is made perfect in weakness.' Therefore, I will boast all the more gladly about my weaknesses, so that Christ's power may rest on me.* -2 Corinthians 12:9 NIV

You must rely on God for everything, and not just your effectiveness. Simply on your ability because it is straightforward for you to walk in your flesh and not exercise self-control. Remember that your weakness not only helps develop Christian character but it also deepens your worship. In admitting your faults, you affirm God's strength.

Jesus encouraged His Disciples to begin sowing the word immediately. Works cannot accomplish salvation, and it is only through Jesus Christ by faith. There are immediate and eternal rewards for winning people to Christ. Eternal life is the only investment in life that cannot be taken away by anyone. Christians can make a lasting investment in the Kingdom of God. There is much work to be done, and the time is now.

chapter

4

STUDY
GUIDE

Now that you have given your life to the Lord, Jesus Christ, the devil is mad. The reason why he is angry is that you are no longer serving him. no longer heading for destruction, just like him. Now that you have received eternal life, there will be temptations, trials, and tribulations coming your way, but don't lose hope; do not give up because Jesus tells us. *³³I have told you these things so that in me you may have peace. In this world, you will have trouble. But take heart! I have overcome the world. -John 16:33 NIV*

Jesus will not abandon you in your time of struggles. Remember that the ultimate victory has already been won on the cross and his resurrection, so you can claim the peace of God that Jesus has given us. *²⁷Peace I leave with you; my peace I give you. I do not give to you as the world gives. Do not let your hearts be troubled and do not be afraid. -John 14:27 NIV*

To better understand the struggles that all Christian go through, you will need to study each battle for *seven days* because in seven days, you will have a better understanding of it and how to overcome them. The reason for looking at each one for seven days is because the bible tells us that the number seven means

completion. In seven days, the world was completed; God has done his work. *¹Thus the heavens and the earth were completed in all their vast array. ²By the seventh day, God had finished the work he had been doing; so on the seventh day, he rested from all his work. ³Then God blessed the seventh day and made it holy because on it he rested from all the work of creating that he had done. -Genesis 2:1-3 NIV*

There are questions to answer in your daily study; the only way to be delivered from your struggles is, to be honest, when answering the question. You must be honest with yourself and to God so that he can set you free from this bondage.

chapter

5

FORGIVENESS

Day 1

[17] Therefore, if anyone is in Christ, the new creation has come.
The old has gone, the new is here! -2 Corinthians 5:17

Before you can forgive anyone, you must first learn how to forgive yourself of your past mistakes because you are a new person. God has forgiven you, so you must do the same to yourself.

What revelation did the Holy Spirit give you about this verse?

_____

_____

_____

_____

What do you need to forgive yourself of?

_____

_____

_____

_____

PRAYER

Lord, I thank you for giving me
of all my sin, and now I'm asking
you to help me to forgive myself
that I'll be able to forgive others.
In Jesus's name, I pray.

Day 2

23 For all have sinned and fall short of the glory of God.

-Romans 3:23 NIV

No one is perfect; Jesus was the only perfect man because he had no sin. You must stop looking back on your past and look at what God is doing in your life. Some sins, seem bigger than others, but they all have the same consequences.

What revelation did the Holy Spirit give you about this verse?

_____

_____

_____

_____

I have to stop beating myself up over?

_____

_____

_____

_____

PRAYER

Lord, I thank you for your
compassion and your Grace
you have become my salvation.
In Jesus's name, I pray.

Day 3

⁵Then I acknowledged my sin to you and did not cover up my iniquity. I said, "I will confess my transgressions to the Lord. And you forgave the guilt of my sin. -Psalm 32:5 NIV

To ask God for forgiveness of your sin is to agree with God, acknowledging that he is the only one that can declare you not guilty of corruption and he is the only one that can restore you.

What revelation did the Holy Spirit give you about this verse?

_____

_____

_____

Do you believe that you are still a sinner and in need of salvation?

_____

_____

_____

_____

PRAYER

God of salvation, fill me with
your assurance that you have
forgiven me, strengthen me, and
hear my prayer. In Jesus's name,
I pray.

Day 4

14For if you forgive other people when they sin against you, your heavenly father will also forgive you. 15But if you do not forgive others their sins, your father will not forgive your sins.
-Matthew 6:14-15 NIV

Jesus has given you a warning about forgiveness. If you refuse to forgive others, God will also refuse to forgive you of your sin. It is easy to ask God for forgiveness but challenging to grant it to others.

What revelation did the Holy Spirit give you about this verse?

_____

_____

_____

Who have you hurt? _____

Who has done you wrong that you must forgive?

_____

_____

_____

PRAYER

Lord, forgive me of my sin, as
I also forgive those who have
sinned against me. In Jesus's
name, I pray.

Day 5

As far as the east is from the west, so far has he removed our transgressions from us. -Psalm 103:12 NIV

When God forgives you of your sin, he separates it from you and does not even remember it. God has wiped your record clean, and that is the same way we must be. When you forgive another, you must also forget the sin; otherwise, you have not honestly forgiven them.

What revelation did the Holy Spirit give you about this verse?

_____

_____

_____

_____ I forgive you for what you did to me.

_____

_____

_____

PRAYER

Lord, I have received your forgiveness and, by the power of the Holy Spirit, give me the strength that I may forgive _____ for _____, and help me not to bring it back up again. Please help me to put it away from me as far as the east is from the west.

In Jesus' name.

Day 6

³²Be kind and compassionate to one another, forgiving each other, just as Christ God forgave you. -Ephesians 4:32 NIV

This is the command that God has given us. God has forgiven you because of his great mercy. As you come to understand his mercy, you will want to be more like him, full of compassion and mercy.

What revelation did the Holy Spirit give you about this verse?

_____

_____

_____

What does compassion mean to you?

_____

Who do you have to show compassion to?

_____

For what reason?

_____

PRAYER

Lord, help me to have
compassion for those who have
hurt me and forgive them just as
Christ Jesus has forgiven me.
In Jesus' name.

Day 7

25 And when you stand praying, if you hold anything against anyone, forgive them, so that your Father in heaven may forgive you your sins. -Mark 11:25 NIV

Forgiving others is challenging work, so much so that many people would instead do something distasteful than offer forgiveness to someone who has wronged them. Before you go before the Lord in prayer and you know that you have wrong someone, make sure that you ask them to forgive you so that your prayer will not be hindered, and if you can't ask them forgiveness, then ask God to forgive you for what you have done to them, and them ask him to forgive you of your sin.

What revelation did the Holy Spirit give you about this verse?

_____

_____

Who are you holding things against?

_____

PRAYER

Lord, I humbly come before your throne of Grace, asking you to forgive me for causing _____ to be hurt and forgive me of all my sins that I have committed against you Today. In Jesus' name.

chapter

6

MERCY

Day 1

⁵⁰His mercy extends to those who fear him, from generation to generation. -Luke 1:50 NIV

Mercy- compassion or forgiveness is shown toward someone within one's power to punish or harm.

God does not punish us as our sins deserve because of Jesus; we receive mercy from God and delivered from judgment. In Jesus, we receive eternal salvation and forgiveness of our sins.

What revelation did the Holy Spirit give you about this verse?

_____

_____

_____

_____

Who do you need to show mercy?

_____

PRAYER

Have mercy on me, O God, according to
your unfailing love; according to your great
compassion, blot out my transgressions.
Wash away all my iniquity and cleanse me
from my sin. -Psalm 51:1-2 NIV

Day 2

¹⁴David said to Gad, 'I am in deep distress. Let us fall into the hands of the LORD, for his mercy is great; but do not let me fall into human hands.' -2 Samuel 24:14 NIV

Even in God's anger, he is more merciful than man. Humans will rather see you suffer for your sin rather than be compassionate. God's wrath lasted only for a moment, but man, it lasts forever.

What revelation did the Holy Spirit give you about this verse?

_____

_____

_____

_____

Think about a time when you should have shown mercy, but instead you use anger in your diction?

_____

_____

_____

_____

PRAYER

Lord, help me be merciful to those who has wronged me, as you have shown me mercy for my sins. In Jesus' name.

Day 3

36Be merciful, just as your father is merciful. -Luke 3:36 NIV

You should love your enemies and show them mercy, just like your heavenly father has shown you.

What revelation did the Holy Spirit give you about this verse?

_____

_____

_____

_____

Who do you need to show mercy?

_____

PRAYER

[3]Have mercy on me, Lord, for I call to you all day long. [4]Bring joy to your servant, Lord, for I put my trust in you. [5]You, Lord, are forgiving and good, abounding in love to all who call to you. [6]Hear my prayer, Lord ; listen to my cry for mercy. -Psalm 86:3-6 NIV

Day 4

⁵He saved us, not because of righteous things we had done, but because of his mercy. He saved us through the washing of rebirth and renewal by the Holy Spirit, ⁶who he poured out us generously through Jesus Christ our Savior. -Titus 3:5-6 NIV

You have a new life through Jesus Christ, and now you are considered righteous not because of what you have done but because of His mercy toward you. There is nothing you can do to earn it nor do you deserve it, and it is all a gift from God.

What revelation did the Holy Spirit give you about this verse?

_____

_____

_____

_____

What do you need to ask God to have mercy on you for?

_____

_____

_____

_____

PRAYER

[20]We wait in hope for the LORD; he is our help and our shield. [21]In him, our hearts rejoice, for we trust in his holy name. [22]May your unfailing love be with us, Lord, even as we put our hope in you.

-Psalm 33:20-22 NIV

Day 5

12For I will be merciful to their unrighteousness, and their sins and their lawless deeds I will remember no more.
-Hebrews 8:12 NKJ

The Lord has forgiven you of your sins and your wickedness, and he will not bring it back up or hold it against you as a man would. Once you ask God for forgiveness and he forgives you, he will not remember it because of his great compassion and love.

What revelation did the Holy Spirit give you about this verse?

_____

_____

_____

I need to show mercy to

_____

PRAYER

⁷I will be glad and rejoice in your
love, for you saw my affliction
and knew the anguish of my soul.

-Psalm 31:7 NIV

Day 6

16Let us then approach God's throne of grace with confidence, so that we may receive mercy and find grace to help us in our time of need. -Hebrews 4:16 NIV

When you pray to the Lord, you must pray with confidence and reverence him because he is your King and Lord. Jesus has paid the price for your sins, so now you have full access to the throne of grace and mercy.

What revelation did the Holy Spirit give you about this verse?

_____

_____

_____

If your enemy come to you and ask you for your mercy, can you show them mercy? _____

If no, why not? _____

_____

If you are having a hard time showing mercy to others, then ask God to help you.

PRAYER

Heavenly Father, I boldly come to
your throne of Grace, asking you to help
me to show mercy to my enemy like you have
shown me, and have compassion on them
like you have compassion on me because
you are my Lord and savior. In Jesus' name.

Day 1

3Praise be to the God and Father of our Lord Jesus Christ! In his great mercy he has given us new birth into a living hope through the resurrection of Jesus Christ from the dead. -1 Peter 1:3 NIV

All the praise and glory belong to Jesus Christ for your salvation. You cannot be a Christian without a fresh beginning based on the salvation that Christ brings. To be born again is a magnificent gift from God and not of works and anything you have done.

What revelation did the Holy Spirit give you about this verse?

_____

_____

_____

Can you remember when you receive mercy from another person? If yes, who _____

For what? _____

How did you feel? _____

If the shoe were on the other foot, could you show the same mercy to that person? _____

PRAYER

My Lord and Savior, I know that your
goodness and mercy shall follow me all
the days of my life because of your love
toward me, and I will serve you, and I
dwell in your house forever. Amen

chapter

7

PRIDE

Day 1

¹⁸Pride goes before destruction, a haughty spirit before a fall.

-Proverbs 16:18 NIV

Proud people think they are above the frailties of everyday people. A prideful person seldom realizes that Pride is their problem. A prideful person will destroy themselves before asking for help from anyone.

What revelation did the Holy Spirit give you about this verse?

_____

_____

_____

_____

Are you struggling with Pride? _____

PRAYER

Lord, help me not to walk in the
Spirit of Pride but humility, knowing
everything I have comes from you and
not of my own doing.
In Jesus' name.

Day 2

^{12}Before a downfall the heart is haughty, but humility comes before honor. -Proverbs 18:12 NIV

When you find yourselves inordinately proud of what you have accomplished. When you do not give thanks to the Lord, your trustworthy source of strength and accomplishment. He is the one who gave you the abilities and opportunities. Pride is self-centered, while humility is a God-centered perspective on life because; without him, you cannot do anything.

What revelation did the Holy Spirit give you about this verse?

_____

_____

_____

_____

Do you find it hard when someone give you suggestions or tell you what to do? _____

If yes, why? _____

_____

PRAYER

Lord, help me to be like what your
word tells me in Roman 12:16, 'Live in
harmony with one another. Do not be
proud but be willing to associate
with people of low position.
Do not be conceited.'
In the name of Jesus.

Day 3

⁴In his Pride the wicked man does not seek him; in all his thoughts there is no room for God. -Psalm 10:4 NIV

A proud person is so consumed with themselves that their thoughts are far from God. In their heart, they have everything, and there is no room for God in their heart. They are blinded by their pride, so that they have no need of God and that God should accept them.

What revelation did the Holy Spirit give you about this verse?

_____

_____

_____

_____

Are you easily offended? _____

If yes, why? _____

_____

PRAYER

Lord, help me to be completely humble and gentle; be patient, bearing with one another in love. -Ephesians 4:2 NIV, and not get offended when I am corrected. In Jesus' name.

Day 4

²When pride comes, then comes disgrace, but with humility comes wisdom. -Proverbs 11:2 NIV

Pride is self-worship that will make you give yourselves credit for something that God has accomplished through you, and Pride will make you take all the glory for yourself that is belongs to God.

What revelation did the Holy Spirit give you about this verse?

_____

_____

_____

Do you look for opportunities to talk about your accomplishments and success? _____

If yes, how to you feel talking about them?

_____

_____

How do you think God feels knowing that you did not give him the credit?

_____

_____

PRAYER

Lord, help me put you first in
everything that I do because I can
accomplish nothing without you, but
with you, I can do all things in
Christ who strengthens me.
In Jesus' name.

Day 5

²³Pride brings a person low, but the lowly in spirit gain honor.
-Proverbs 29:23 NIV

When you are arrogant, vain, and prideful, you will not grow in favor with God are with men. No man wants to be around someone who all way talks about themself, and they will do what they can to cut you off from friendships are even open any door to give you opportunities. When you are humble, modest, and submissive, God enjoys your Spirit, and He will exalt you to a higher position, and you will find favor with man and appreciate you, and do what they can include and promote you.

What revelation did the Holy Spirit give you about this verse?

_____

_____

_____

Do you rely on you own abilities rather than seek God for his help? _____

If yes, why? _____

_____

PRAYER

Lord, help me not to be prideful that I miss
your blessing but allow me to do what your
word tell me in Isaiah 66:2: 'These are the ones
I look on with favor: those who are humble and
contrite in spirit, and who tremble at my word'
so that I can look upon myself with favor.
In Jesus' name.

Day 6

³If anyone thinks they are something when they are not, they deceive themselves. -Galatians 6:3 NIV

It's very dangerous when you start to feel yourself too much because you will lose sight of God and started to think you are in control. If you are going to boast, then boast only in the Lord! Not in your ability.

What revelation did the Holy Spirit give you about this verse?

_____

_____

_____

_____

Do you think that you are entitled to more because of your achievements? _____

Are do you think that you are better than them? _____

PRAYER

[1]Lord , I have given up my Pride and turned away from my arrogance. I am not concerned with significant matters or subjects too difficult for me. [2]Instead, I am content and at peace. As a child lies quietly in its mother's arms, so my heart is quiet within me. -Psalm 131:1-2 NIV. In Jesus' name.

Day 7

⁵The LORD detests all the proud of heart. Be sure of this: they will not go unpunished. -Proverbs 16:5 NIV

God sees the Pride that other people don't see in your heart, and obviously it is the inward Pride that brings out outward expressions. God knows the core and thoughts of every human being, He knows the arrogant, and He despises them.

What revelation did the Holy Spirit give you about this verse?

_____

_____

_____

_____

Do you do things to be seen? _____

Do you conceal it, or do you hope people see you and compliment you? _____

If yes to both questions, you have Pride in your heart.

PRAYER

Lord, help me with the sin of Pride that is in my heart, take it away from me, and replace it with the Spirit of humility so I can please you and give you all the glory in everything that I do. I need you in my life because without you, I'm nothing. In Jesus' name.

chapter

8

FAITH

Day 7

11Now faith is confidence in what we hope for and assurance about what we do not see. -Hebrews 11:1 NIV

Believing that God will fulfill his promises even though we don't see those promises yet.

What revelation did the Holy Spirit give you about this verse?

_____

_____

_____

_____

Do you think that the bible is figurative or literal? _____

Figurative why? _____

Literal why? _____

PRAYER

Lord Jesus, help me with my
unbelief so that I can trust in you
in all your promises and bless me
with understanding of your word,
help me to know you better, and
strengthen my faith in you. In
Jesus' name.

Day 2

⁶And without faith it is impossible to please God, because anyone who comes to him must believe that he exists and that he rewards those who earnestly seek him. -Hebrews 11:6 NIV

Faith is the only thing that you have because you have not seen Jesus Christ. Faith is all about your heart that you know that there is a God, and he loves you so much that He sent Jesus to die for us. If you don't believe in the Son, you can't please God no matter how good you are or how much you can do a certain thing good.

What revelation did the Holy Spirit give you about this verse?

_____

_____

Do you think God answer prayers? _____

If no, why? _____

_____

If yes, why? _____

_____

PRAYER

Lord, I humbly come before your
throne of Grace, thanking you for
answering my prayers.
In Jesus' name.

Day 3

⁸For it is by Grace you have been saved, through faith—and this is not from yourselves, it is the gift of God. -Ephesians 2:8 NIV

Some Christians, even after they have received the gift of salvation, feel obligated to work their way to God. Your salvation and even your faith are a gift from God; you should respond with gratitude and joy.

What revelation did the Holy Spirit give you about this verse?

_____

_____

_____

_____

If you could know God personally, would you want to?

_____

_____

_____

_____

PRAYER

Lord, I desire to have a closer
relationship with you, like you did
with Adam, then we can reason
together so I can look upon your glory.
In Jesus' name.

Day 4

*¹⁷Consequently, faith comes from hearing the message, and the
message is heard through the Word about Christ.
-Romans 10:17 NIV*

The more you hear the word and the more you read the Word of
God, the more your faith will be strengthened. The more you hear
the word, the more you will begin to trust God because without
trust your faith will be weak. Trust and loyalty go together.

What revelation did the Holy Spirit give you about this verse?

_____

_____

_____

_____

What experience in your life that has challenge your faith?

_____

_____

_____

_____

PRAYER

Lord, I thank you for the trial you brought me out of because it has strengthen my faith and I am able to trust you even more. In Jesus' name.

Day 5

⁵Who through faith are shielded by God's power until the coming of the salvation that is ready to be revealed in the last time.
-1 Peter 1:5 NIV

Faith must be more than belief in specific facts, and it must result in action, growth in Christian character, and the practice of moral discipline.

What revelation did the Holy Spirit give you about this verse?

_____

_____

_____

_____

Are you walking in faith or fear? _____

If is fear, why?

_____

_____

_____

PRAYER

Lord, hear my prayer, listen to my cry for mercy, help me with my fear because you did not give me the Spirit of fear, but I'm struggling with anxiety, thank you for delivering me from the Spirit of fear. In Jesus' name.

Day 6

10 Clearly no one who relies on the law is justified before God, because "the righteous will live by faith. -Galatians 3:11 NIV

Trusting God's Word and living a life that is entirely dependent upon Him for everything. You can't be justified in the sight of God through works of the law.

What revelation did the Holy Spirit give you about this verse?

_____

_____

_____

_____

What is your relationship with God? _____

By the law? _____

Are by faith? _____

PRAYER

Lord, Let the morning bring me word of your unfailing love, for I have put my trust in you. Please show me the way I should go, for to you I entrust my life. In Jesus' name.

Day 7

¹⁷For in the gospel the righteousness of God is revealed—a righteousness that is by faith from first to last, just as it is written: 'The righteous will live by faith.' -Romans 1:17 NIV

By trusting in Jesus Christ, our relationship with God is made right, from start to finish; God declares us to be right with him because of faith and faith alone.

What revelation did the Holy Spirit give you about this verse?

_____

_____

_____

_____

How important is it for you to live by faith?

_____

_____

_____

_____

PRAYER

Lord, I trust you like your word tells me. ³Trust in the Lord and do good; dwell in the land and enjoy safe pasture.

⁴Take delight in the Lord , and he will give you the desires of your heart. - Psalm 37:3-4 NIV. In Jesus' name.

Notes